"Dream of mountains as in their sleep,
they brood of things eternal."
– C.A. Higgins

First Edition

Text & Photos © 2021 Steven Kelman

ISBN 978-1-7357679-7-0

www.bunburysbooks.com

Piermont:
Where the mountain meets the marsh

~

Words & Photographs by Steve Kelman

BUNBURY'S
BB
BOOKS
PIERMONT, N.Y.

The author would like to thank the following people: My publisher and editor Debra Pirsos for her guidance with this project, her son Chris, for being a second set of eyes, the staff at Bunbury's, and Ned Kelly for the support and encouragement that got me going last year.

Dedicated to my parents Sue and Edward.

Marsh reflections taken on a late afternoon from the walking path into Tallman Mountain State Park

It can be said that the picturesque village of Piermont is where the mountain meets the marsh. Here the waters of the Sparkill Creek empty into the Hudson River and the 171 foot Tallman Mountain towers over the town.

Tallman Mountain is also the name of a 700 plus acre state park that abuts and includes the Piermont Marsh. The marsh "occupies two miles of shoreline just south of the Piermont Pier including the creek and extensive tidal shallows." [1] DEC website

There are in fact 1017 acres of wetlands that make up this portion of the Hudson River National Estuarine Reserve, one of four sites along the river, between here and Albany.

The other locations are Iona Island, Tivoli Bays, and Stockport Flats.

Now Piermont has always been a special place for me for many reasons. And it has been the place where I have spent a good deal of time outside walking and thus taking photographs during this pandemic.

As of late I have paid special close attention to the marshlands abutting Tallman Mountain State Park and Paradise Avenue in the village.

I have also observed the marshlands by walking the mile-long pier, half-way out into the Hudson River, from the top of the state park and in the little community of Bogertown as well.

View of the marsh, creek and mountain from Bogertown.

Dating back to the early 19th century, Bogertown today consists of a group of ten interesting and quaint houses, really a small waterfront neighborhood where the marsh is the backyard and sometimes, after a drenching rain, the front yard as well.

The area was once known as Tappan Landing and "The Slote," which is from the Dutch meaning **ditch**. Bogertown is named for the prominent residents of this community, the Bogert Family who settled in the area circa, 1824, according to the historic marker placed on Paradise Avenue.

As previously stated, Tallman Mountain State Park consists of 700 acres and "comprises wooded country on the easterly sloop of the Palisades uplands overlooking the Hudson and the Piermont Marsh which lies between the river and the slope."
[2] parks.ny.gov/119/details.aspx

Diary Entry #1
December 23, 2020

Numerous noisy blue jays, the rattle of a Kingfisher and the "Cheer" notes of the Northern Cardinal provided the soundtrack today as I took photographs of the marsh.

Proceeding along Paradise Avenue I observed a group of Mallard Ducks resting Creekside along a wooden wall, located on the property owned by one of the road's homeowners.

Diary Entry #2
January 16, 2021

There was water, water almost everywhere this morning as I walked by the creek, and specifically adjacent to Ferdon and Paradise Avenues.

Torrential rains from the night before brought flooding to properties both private and wild. Some roadways were also inundated with rising flood waters especially at Bogertown and near the Bridge Street Bridge.

It certainly was a good day to be a duck as they were out in force, enjoying the limited sunshine and warm temperatures (Upper 40s, not bad for mid January.)

There was a bonanza of ambient light which reflected nicely along the creek, thus providing some interesting photo opportunities.

Diary Entry #3
January 17, 2021

The water has disappeared from the areas that were flooded not even 24 hours ago, an almost total evaporation! At Bogertown, front yards have returned and cars can once again navigate the roadway.

Here is a list of birds that I have either observed by sight or ear (mostly by ear) during this ongoing pandemic.

Bald Eagle - Pier in July	Crows	Starlings	Tufted Titmouse
Cat Birds	Fish Crows	Mallards	Flicker
Northern Mockingbird	Cardinal	Canada Goose	Peregrine Falcon
Kingfisher	Turkey Vulture	White Throated Sparrows	Eastern Woods Pewee
Grackles	Carolina Wren	Red Winged Blackbirds	Egrets
Robins	Downy Woodpecker	Mourning Doves	Cormorant
	House Finches		

In previous seasons I have also observed seals off of the pier during summer and during one winter season many years ago, a snowy owl. Here are observations from a late morning walk back on June 17, 2020.

Cormorant	Red Wing Blackbirds	Cardinal	Canada Goose
Egrets	White Throated Sparrow	Black Vultures (3)	Mallards
Great Blue Heron	Carolina Wren	House Sparrows	Grackles
		Robins	

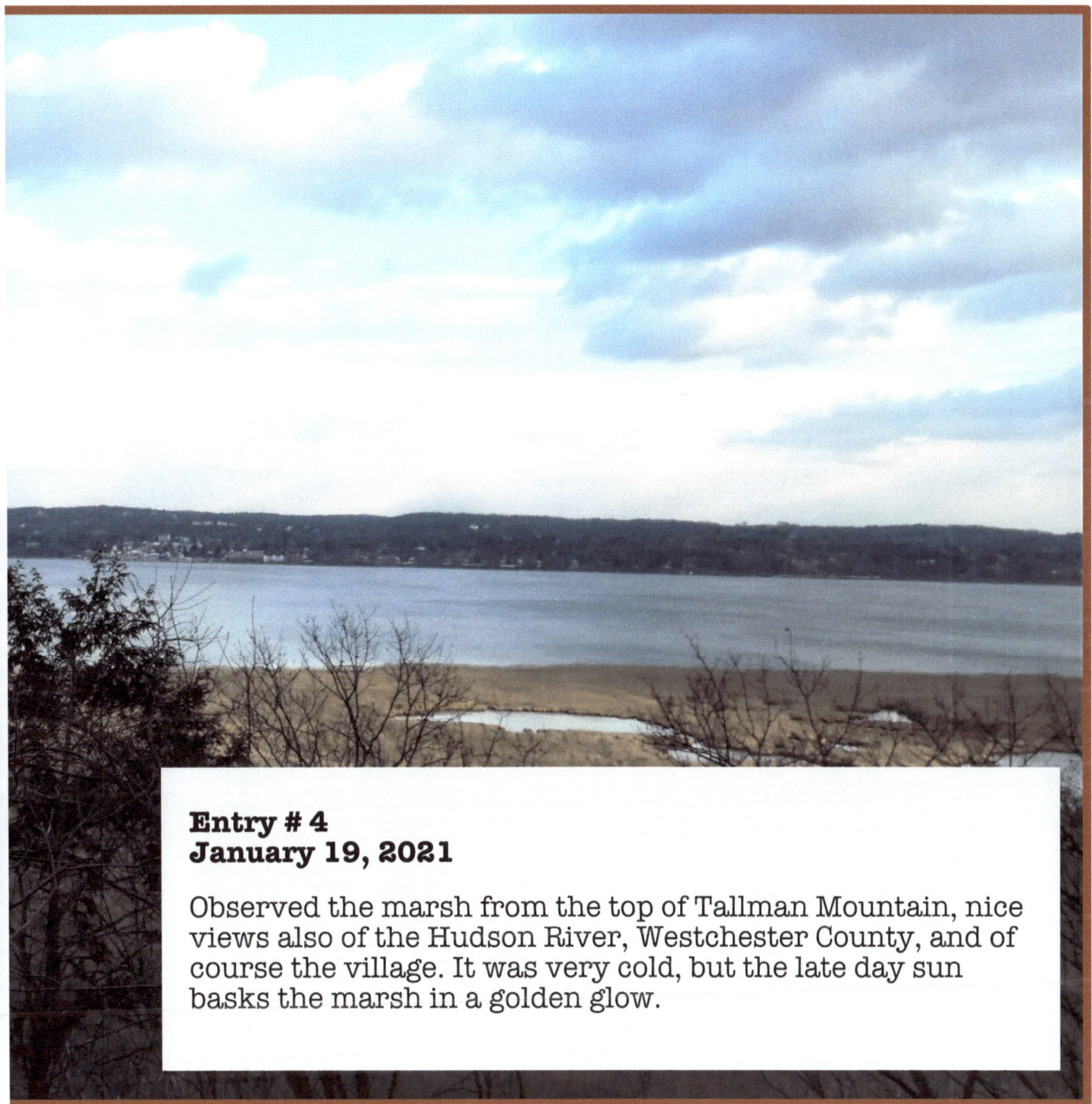

Entry # 4
January 19, 2021

Observed the marsh from the top of Tallman Mountain, nice views also of the Hudson River, Westchester County, and of course the village. It was very cold, but the late day sun basks the marsh in a golden glow.

Entry #5
January 21, 2021

On the day after the inauguration of our nation's 46th president I decided to get up close and personal with the marsh. From different vantage points on the pier and at a pond that I never knew existed located just beyond the village baseball field.

At these locations I photographed ice, phragmites, rock, river, dead fish and a peregrine falcon.

As I proceeded towards the pier I was serenaded by catbirds and black capped chickadees. The falcon, which was brought to my attention by a woman driving by, was perched high up in a tree near the pier entrance looking for lunch I'm sure.

Before telling me about the falcon, this woman asked me if I was photographing anything interesting, I told her that depended on what she would consider interesting. And that was when she told me where to look for the bird. Being able to locate and then photograph that falcon was certainly the high point of the day. Later as I walked back along Paradise Avenue I heard the rattle of the Kingfisher along with the shriek of a Red Tail Hawk off in the distance.

Peregrine Falcon

Musical Reflections...

"May the Salvation Army be your Turning Point." This inspirational slogan was posted on a storefront in the fictional downtown setting, a part of Woody Allen's 1985 movie, **The Purple Rose of Cairo** that was filmed in the village.

The storefront was in fact located directly next to the popular music venue of the same name which featured live entertainment for over three decades until the pandemic hit.

The Turning Point music scene provided a soundtrack for much of my life culturally speaking. Starting as a small cafe that could hold no more than 36 people, it was the only place I knew where a teenager could go to for musical entertainment and not be turned away due to his or her age. Back then I remember ordering a cheese board from their menu consisting of different cheeses, apples and Italian bread for a mere $ 2.00. The first folks who played there did it for tips, a wine carafe was passed around from table to table.

I later attended the first concert performances there, shows featuring folksinger Eric Anderson and folk legend Ramblin Jack Elliott back in 1984. What follows is only a partial list of the performing artists who have played this venerable venue...

Arlo Guthrie

Kris Kristofferson

Levon Helm

Rick Danko

Richie Havens

New Riders of the Purple Sage

Dr. John

Taj Mahal

David Bromberg

Jorma Kaukonen

Pine Top Perkins

Robert Cray

John Hartford

Tom Chapin

Christine Lavin

Dave Mason

John Mayall

Bill Monroe and His Bluegrass Boys

Dan Hicks and His Hot Licks

Debbie Davies

Danny Kalb

Roy Bookbinder

Paul Geremia

Townes Van Zandt

Kenny Rankin

John Gorka

And now...
A Night at the Turning Point staring William Hurt....

Sometime back during the mid 1980s, an Academy Award winning actor, William Hurt, was residing near Piermont. When he was not on location making films, he would occasionally spend some of his down time in Piermont at the Turning Point.

On one such weeknight evening that featured some long forgotten local band I observed Hurt sitting at the bar flirting with a local lady. I was sitting across from him on another barstool, but with my back turned away from him watching the show. During the band's intermission Hurt got up and walked out of the club leaving a large envelope at his seat. What did it contain? no doubt a script for an upcoming film he was working on (think **Children of a Lesser God** or **Broadcast News**.)

No matter, I seized the initiative went over to where he was sitting, seized the large envelope real stealth like and followed the actor to his car which was parked in front of the venue. Hurt was feeling no pain it seemed, anyway I knocked on his window and handed him his envelop. He grabbed it and mumbled something that I could not quite make out, maybe a thank you, and then drove off.

~ The End ~

Other Turning Point moments...

Hanging out with Texas Blues Guitarist Johnny "Clyde" Copeland before his two set show one summer evening and talking to him about several other local gigs he and his band had recently played, one of which was at the Hudson River Clearwater Festival.

*

Buying a glass of whiskey for legendary blues piano player Pinetop Perkins, who in turn gave me his business card, which I still have and treasure.

*

Seeing a down and out, little known Texas singer/songwriter by the name of Townes Van Zandt play before a crowd of six people counting myself. To be truthful I never heard of him at the time and only attended because I won tickets for the show from a local college radio station. He proceeded to get very drunk, which sadly, was his MO. Van Zandt is best known for his song, "Pancho and Lefty" considered a song writing masterpiece and covered by such artists as Emmylou Harris, Willie Nelson and Merle Haggard. He died in 1997.

Another side trip down memory lane:
Missing those "Old Man" bars

Now that it seems that I'm headed in the direction of becoming one (getting older by the second), I reflect back to an earlier day when there was an "old man" bar on what seemed like every corner.

OK that is a slight exaggeration but just about every town along the New York border had at least one such establishment. These places were working class, blue collar bars, (they were not called old man bars at the time) not to be confused with the trendier night club discos that were all the rage in the mid to late 1970s and then into the 1980s.

In Northern Bergen County there were watering holes with such names as the Taz Bar and "The Wreck" in Closter, Tatter Toms in Cresskill, and Stein and Steer in Norwood.

In New York, Tappan had two such establishments, the Oak Tree Inn and Sullivan's. Sparkill had Bilbos, and Orangeburg had the Side Porch.

And Piermont offered more than its fair share of watering holes, with four, all within easy walking distance of each other.

They were Dave's Bar, Crackerbox, the Piermont Pub and Mom Miraglias. While each of these places were unique, one thing they all had in common was that the consumer had the opportunity to drink very cheaply.

At the Corner Bar, a place where I was able to walk to for example, I remember being able to drink 8-ounce glasses of Budweiser for $.35 each.

Most of these watering holes also offered a number of other amenities such as pinball machines, pool tables, dart boards, etc. There was a billiards table at the Oak Tree Inn in Tappan, and even a bowling alley at "The Wreck" in Closter.

Several nights a week The Crackerbox offered live entertainment, usually a solo guitar player or combo, performing for rough blue collar crowds.

I happened to be one of those performers and had more than a few adventures playing there. There was the night for example that a lady brought in her parrot and placed the bird on my shoulder as I was rendering a cover version of the Lennon and McCarthy classic "Black Bird." And yes, that parrot did relieve itself on my arm before the song was over, I did somehow get through it.

I also had at least one regular fan, the town drunk, who would every time he saw me play take out his keys and try to play percussion. He would also dangle his keys in my face, this always got laughs from my friends and other patrons.

Back before I was legally able to drink my friends and I would go to the Turning Point, usually on a Sunday night. Many times we would have to wait next store at Dave's Bar for a table there to become available. The bartender would only sell us soda or juice while we waited. Occasionally we could get in a game of pool before an opening became available. The Turning Point at the time in its first location had a legal capacity of 36 people as mentioned earlier.

When the COVID-19 pandemic hit back in March of 2020, it felt like I was punched in the stomach and mugged. There was not much to do, so I stayed home at first and completed a lot of yard and house related projects. As time went by depression reared its ugly head. And with good reason, I lost virtually all of my performing gigs along with my other work.

And when I started to venture out it was to Piermont, spending many hours first just sitting on the bench located near the Tappan Zee Thrift Shop.

It was a good day when the local coffee shop Bunbury's reopened. I believe it was in early June. Then I could at least sit on said bench with a cup of hazelnut or French Roast to sip and watch the world go by. Soon I began walking the village, the pier, then into Tallman State Park. This would take up a good part of the day. It was not long until I started on a regular basis bringing my camera along, a practice that I still do even as this book is coming together.

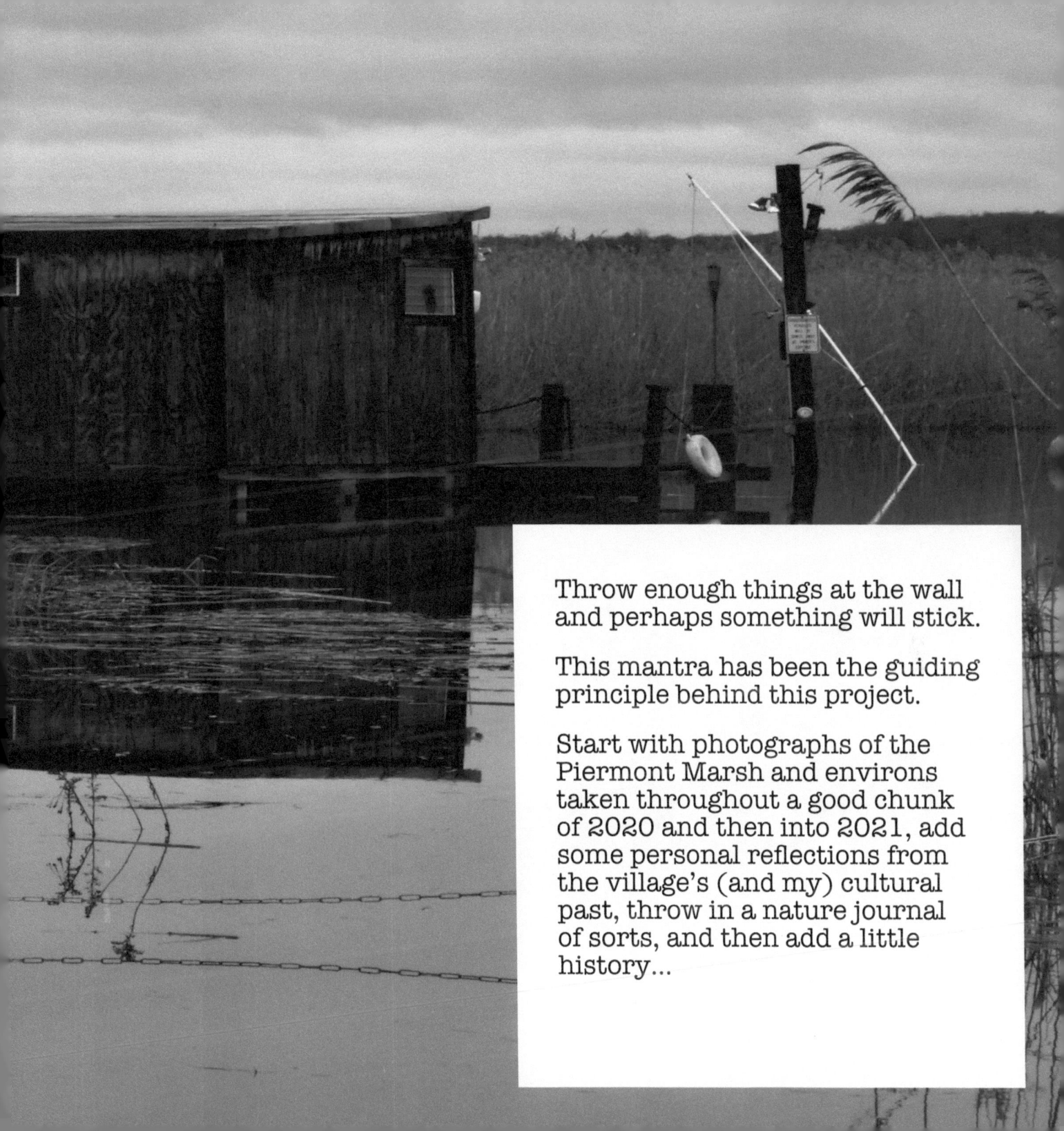

Throw enough things at the wall and perhaps something will stick.

This mantra has been the guiding principle behind this project.

Start with photographs of the Piermont Marsh and environs taken throughout a good chunk of 2020 and then into 2021, add some personal reflections from the village's (and my) cultural past, throw in a nature journal of sorts, and then add a little history...

Leave it Alone!

Back in 1903 when the 26th President of the United States and a former Governor of New York State Theodore Roosevelt visited the Grand Canyon he gave a speech in which he urged the American people not to attempt any man-made improvements to the site. "Leave it as it is...the ages have been at work on it and only man can mare it." Now the same can be true of the 4000-year-old Piermont Marsh.

Plans to dose and kill the phragmites with chemicals should never move forward in my humble opinion. And I am not alone. Residents against the plan have said they believed that the phragmites helped to protect the village from significant damage during Hurricanes Irene and Sandy.

In 1987 the marsh was designated a "significant coastal fish and wildlife habitat" by the New York Department of State, (NYDOS.)

The designation was given, "in recognition of ecosystem rarity, the presence of vulnerable wildlife species, its regional significance for human use and an unusual concentration of wildlife and fish species in the area." This designation is included in the December 2017 Draft Piermont Marsh Reserve Management Plan.

I will not go on. Put very simply the marsh is a special place on many levels and it should be left alone.

"In every
walk with nature
one receives far more
than he seeks."

– John Muir

I'll end however, with this disclaimer: this little book is not meant to be a history of Piermont or of the 4000 year old marsh, although there are some elements of this, and it is not a biography of my life, something that no one, myself included, would really want to read.

But offered here are some personal insights and notes from past and current experiences that I think may be interesting, at least this is my hope while in this pandemic time and beyond.

Walking Route #1: Piermont Village/Tallman Mountain State Park/ Bogertown and Paradise Avenue

An easy walk, mostly on village streets plus a gravel path in Tallman Park. Allow 1 hour or so.

Start at the bus stop bench where there is a building (a former law office) with half of a mural painted on it. Cross the street and proceed towards Parking Lot D, which you will pass on the right, then make a right turn onto Paradise Avenue.

Walk towards the marsh, do not make the immediate left turn for the pier at this point. The First Stop is Bogertown. Here there are ten very charming homes that abut the Piermont Marsh. Next proceed along Paradise Avenue.

Stop 2 is "The View." Walk across a small wooden platform (on the left) adjacent to a sign for the National Preserve. From here (there is a small bench and three historic storyboards to read), take in views of Tallman Mountain, the Sparkill Creek, the Piermont Marsh and the backsides of resident homes along the creek.

Then continue walking on Paradise Avenue (avoid walking on the creek side properties, stay on sidewalk instead) until you reach the traffic light and Kane Park (on the left.) Make a left and walk along the wooden sidewalk of the Ferdon Street Bridge for **Stop 3**, offering another view of the creek.

For **Stop 4**, turn Left into Tallman Mountain State Park (look for the information kiosk), walk along the gravel path with views of the marsh on your left and the mountain to your right, until you reach the parking lot for Tallman Pool then turn around and return the same way towards the village.

Note- Hikers may want to follow the blue blazed long path up to the summit of Tallman Mountain and beyond. Consult the New York Walk Book (NYNJ Trail Conference Publications) for information on the Long Path and the route.

From the start of the gravel path in Tallman cross the street towards The Bridge Street Bridge, the oldest known example in the United States of a "simple archaic draw bridge design" This is **Stop 5**, here there are places to sit and take in the view of the Sparkill Creek.

Finish crossing the bridge, walk a short way and make a right at the Post Office, then walk back towards the traffic light. Make a left and continue on the sidewalk a few feet until reaching **Stop 6,** the Last Stop USA memorial which is incidentally the last stop on this walk.

The memorial commemorates the Piermont Pier as the last place where over a million service members boarded ships, then sailed up the Hudson River and over to Europe for action during World War II. The Pier was the last time many of these soldiers would set foot on American soil.

Continue along the sidewalk to the site of the mural building and other shops along Piermont Avenue.

Walking Route #2

The Piermont Pier can be easily accessed from Parking Lot D. This is an easy walk on a level paved roadway, the pier, extends one mile out into the Hudson River with views of Westchester County, the Mario Cuomo Bridge, the marsh, Tallman Mountain and even New Jersey, allow at least an hour to complete.

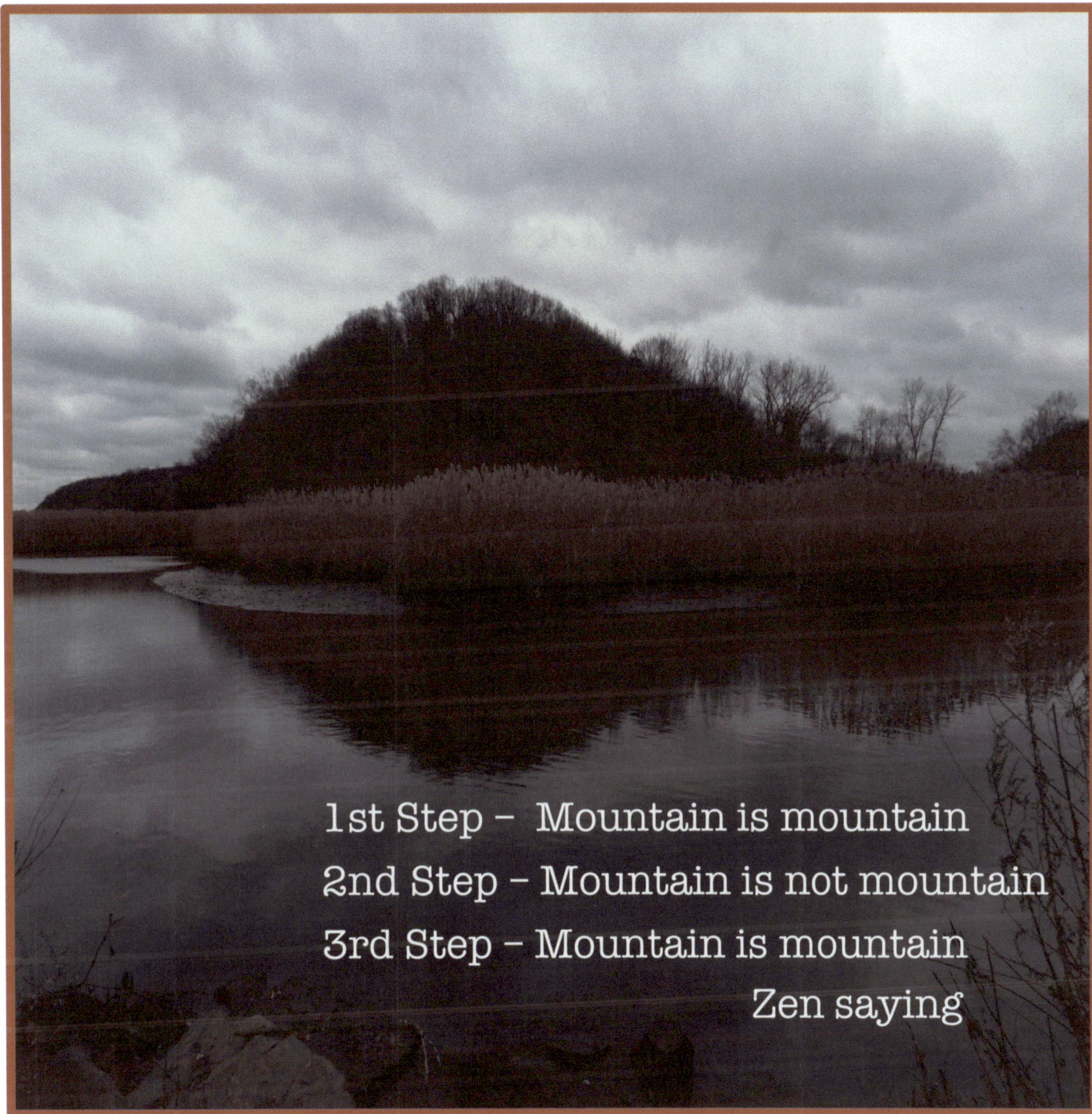

1st Step – Mountain is mountain
2nd Step – Mountain is not mountain
3rd Step – Mountain is mountain

Zen saying

About the Author

Steve Kelman is a journalist, musician and photographer who lives in Northern New Jersey. His writings and photographs have appeared in such publications as the Van Wyck Gazette, Nyack News and Views, and the Press Group Newspapers. Before the pandemic he performed throughout the Hudson River Valley and North Jersey. He hopes to again.

This is his first book.